S ASTONISH   HEADLINES AS

STOWED AWAY

Eric Embacher

SADDLEBACK
EDUCATIONAL PUBLISHING

ASTONISHING HEADLINES

Attacked

Captured

Condemned

Kidnapped

Lost and Found

Missing

Shot Down

Stowed Away

Stranded at Sea

Trapped

SADDLEBACK
EDUCATIONAL PUBLISHING
www.sdlback.com

Copyright © 2005, 2013 by Saddleback Educational Publishing

ISBN-13: 978-1-61651-925-4
ISBN-10: 1-61651-925-8
eBook: 978-1-61247-082-5

Printed in Guangzhou, China
0712/CA21201055

17 16 15 14 13   1 2 3 4 5

Photo Credits: Cover, courtesy of the Coordinating Group on Alien Pest Species, page 37, Bob Pepping, KRT; page 67 © Suljo | Dreamstime.com; page 72, © Olaf Speier | Dreamstime.com; page 85, © Ron Chapple | Dreamstime.com; pages 88–89, © Dylanbz | Dreamstime.com

CONTENTS

A stowaway's trip is very dangerous. He or she might stow away on an airplane, boat, or truck. But the stowaway does not pay for a ticket. Often, he or she cannot afford the fare. If the stowaway is discovered, the police often send him or her to jail.

People have been stowing away for centuries. Balboa is best known for discovering the Pacific Ocean in 1513. But Balboa might never have made his famous find if he had not stowed away on a ship three years earlier.

During the Civil War era, Harriet Tubman drove carts full of stowaway slaves. She took them to the northern states where they would be free.

Edson Rojas was a stowaway in the back of a tractor-trailer from Mexico to the United States in 1992. It was a very dangerous trip. Edson almost died.

In 2003, Charles McKinley could not afford an airplane ticket home to Texas. So he packed himself in a box. He arrived safely at his parent's doorstep!

Even though the trips were dangerous, these brave people felt they had no choice. They had a chance at a better life by stowing away!

People are not the only ones who stow away. Sometimes animals get aboard ships or planes without anyone knowing. This was the case in Guam during the mid 1940s. A few brown tree snakes stowed away on US military ships headed for Guam. Today, the snakes are a huge problem on the tiny island.

Balboa Stows Away in a Barrel
DATAFILE

Timeline

September 1510
Balboa stows away in a barrel.

September 1513
Balboa is the first European to see the Pacific Ocean.

Where is Hispaniola (Haiti)?

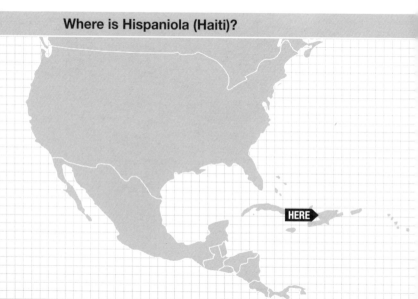

Key Terms

colony—a region ruled by another country

expedition—a group of people working together to make a discovery

?

Did You Know?

Balboa's dog, Leoncico, was huge. It was a cross between a greyhound and a mastiff. Leoncico's nickname was "little lion." It is unclear how Balboa managed to sneak such a large dog aboard Enciso's ship.

Balboa Stows Away in a Barrel

Vasco Núñez de Balboa is one of the world's greatest explorers. However, Balboa was once a stowaway!

Balboa was born in Spain around 1475. He trained to be a soldier from a young age. Growing up, Balboa heard stories of treasure and gold in the new Spanish colonies. In 1501, Balboa joined Don Rodrigo de Bastidas's crew and their two ships. He sailed to the New World with hopes of becoming rich and famous.

Success and Failure

Balboa's first voyage was very successful. He traded goods for pearls and gold. But soon after,

Balboa's ship sank off the coast of Hispaniola. Luckily, most of the gold and pearls were saved. However, Balboa's luck did not last long. The governor of Hispaniola believed Balboa traded illegally with the Indians. As punishment, he took away one third of Balboa's riches. Balboa also spent one month in jail for his crime.

A Farming Life

Balboa did not return to Spain with Bastidas. He settled in Santo Domingo, Hispaniola. Today, we know Hispaniola as Haiti and the Dominican Republic.

For the next seven years, Balboa farmed the land. But he was a bad farmer. Soon, he owed many people large sums of money. With no way to pay his debts, Balboa was desperate to escape Hispaniola.

So, at the age of 35, Balboa and his friend, Bartolomé Hurtado, made a plan. Balboa would become a stowaway!

Escape!

In early September 1510, after much discussion and thought, Balboa and Hurtado decided Balboa would be loaded onto a departing ship in a large barrel. Though it is not certain how he did it, Balboa also took his faithful dog, Leoncico, aboard with him.

It was dark and uncomfortable in the barrel. Once the ship set sail, Balboa crawled out of the barrel. He hid for some time in a spare sail below deck.

Not far off the coast of Hispaniola, Spanish officials looking for stowaways boarded the ship. Balboa could not risk being found. The law prevented people from leaving Santo Domingo without paying off their debts. If Balboa were caught, he might be killed. Luckily, the authorities did not find him.

Caught

Once out to sea, Balboa revealed himself to the crew. The crew quickly told Captain Martín Fernández de Enciso about Balboa. Captain Enciso was furious and wanted to leave Balboa on the next deserted island. However, Balboa's friends among the crew convinced the captain to keep Balboa aboard as a crewman.

With the wind in his hair and his dog, Leoncico, beside him, Balboa was a free man! He sailed on with Captain Enciso's crew until Balboa eventually became a ship captain himself. It was not long after that Balboa led the expedition that eventually discovered the Pacific Ocean!

Balboa Discovers the Pacific Ocean

Indians who lived on present-day Haiti told the Spanish explorers about a southern sea and a land rich in gold. They also told the Spaniards it would take 1,000 men to claim that land for Spain.

On September 1, 1513, Balboa sailed to present-day Panama. With him, Balboa had more than 190 Spanish soldiers and hundreds of Indians.

Some of Balboa's men stayed onshore. The smaller group marched south across Panama, through dense jungles, rivers, and swamps. It was some of the densest rainforest in the world. Throughout the journey, Balboa and his men battled many native tribes.

In 1513, at the end of September, from the top of a mountain range, Balboa saw the Pacific Ocean. He became the first European to look out on the Pacific Ocean from its eastern shore. When his group joined him on top of the mountain, they built a pile of stones and sang a song of celebration.

Four days later, Balboa and his men reached the Pacific Ocean's shore and claimed it and the lands that touched it for Spain. Balboa named this place St. Michael's Bay.

The Spanish spent a month on the shore. They collected pearls and gold from what are now called the Pearl Islands. Balboa returned to Spain in January 1514.

Tubman Stows Away Slaves for Freedom
DATAFILE

Timeline

1849

Harriet Tubman escapes slavery and heads north.

1850–1860

Harriet Tubman rescues more than 300 slaves.

Where was the Underground Railroad?

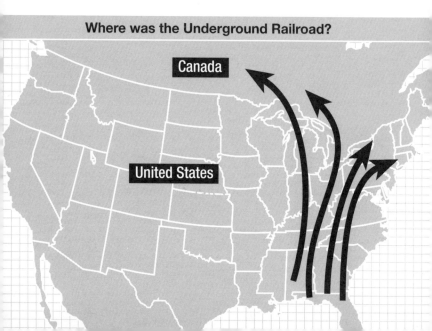

Key Terms

disfigured—deeply scarred, having the appearance spoiled

rebellious—to act out against those in authority

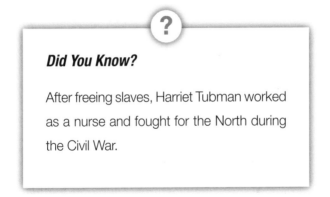

Did You Know?

After freeing slaves, Harriet Tubman worked as a nurse and fought for the North during the Civil War.

Tubman Stows Away Slaves for Freedom

They say you would have never known it to look at her. Small and disfigured, Harriet Tubman did not look anything like the daring escape artist that she was. However, little Harriet Tubman became one of America's first female heroes by stowing away and rescuing more than 300 slaves before the Civil War.

Harriet Tubman was born Araminta Ross in 1820 in Dorchester County, Maryland. Araminta was a slave. She suffered very much during her childhood. At the age of nine, she was whipped five or six times a day by her master.

Scarred for Life

In her teens, an overseer threw a jar or other heavy object at her head when Araminta helped another slave escape a beating. It took her months to recover and she had blackouts, or "sleeping spells," for the rest of her life. Araminta was also left with a large dent in her head and scars from her beatings.

Free at Last!

Araminta changed her first name to Harriet, her mother's first name. In 1844, she married John Tubman. As she grew older, a life of hard work made Harriet very strong. Her master even feared her rebellious nature.

In 1849, Harriet believed she was about to be sold. Soon she made her escape north to Philadelphia—free at last!

"I looked at my hands to see if I was the same person. The Sun came like gold through the trees, and over the fields, and I felt like I was in Heaven." — Harriet Tubman

Harriet was very pleased to be free in the North. However, a part of her felt badly about her family and friends still in slavery in the South.

Underground Railroad

In 1850, Harriet learned about the Underground Railroad. This was a system of houses and hideouts on the journey north where people helped slaves on their way to freedom.

Harriet planned to go back into the South and rescue her family members, one by one. In December 1850, Harriet rescued her sister, Mary Ann, and her family from Baltimore, Maryland. Encouraged by her success, in 1851, Harriet returned to the South to rescue her brother and two other men.

Making trips into the South was somewhat easy. No one expected a slave to head south. Most people thought Harriet was a free woman.

Daring Rescues

When making her daring rescues, Harriet would often take the master's horse and cart. She would load the slaves into the cart and hide them beneath piles of hay or vegetables. Once, Harriet even hid the slaves beneath a pile of manure!

Sometimes the runaway slaves would be afraid. They knew their masters would beat them or even kill them if they got caught. So they would ask Harriet to let them return to the South. But Harriet would not allow it. The fleeing slaves might give away everyone else's whereabouts. Harriet would pull out her pistol and say, "You go on or die!" Later the scared slaves would thank Harriet for her courage in continuing the journey.

Dead or Alive

After her successful rescues, Harriet became quite famous. Many slave owners wanted her dead or alive. There was a $40,000 reward for her capture. That's equal to a million dollars today!

Because of this, Harriet had to be very clever so that she was not caught. Harriet often dressed and acted like an elderly woman. No one suspected she was freeing slaves! She also acted in other unexpected ways. If Harriet and her group came upon a slave owner, she would turn the group around and start heading south. The slave owner believed no slave would willingly head south, so they must be free.

In 1860, Harriet made her final rescue. In 10 years, she had helped rescue more than 300 slaves! Even today, Harriet is remembered as a hero and an inspiration to all because of her cleverness and courage.

Harriet Tubman, a conductor of the Underground Railroad.

Brown Tree Snakes Take Over Guam
DATAFILE

Timeline

1945–1950
Brown tree snakes arrive in Guam stowed away in US military shipments.

1990
There are as many as 30,000 brown tree snakes per square mile in Guam.

Where is Guam?

Key Terms

cargo—goods transported in planes, trucks, ships, etc.

estimate—to make an informed guess about a measurement

nuisance—an annoying problem

predator—an animal that hunts and eats other animals

slither—to slide; to move like a snake

Did You Know?

The brown tree snake's bite is painful. But it is not likely to kill a human. A female snake can lay up to 12 eggs once or twice a year. The eggs hatch 90 days later.

Brown Tree Snakes Take Over Guam

Imagine reading these headlines in your local newspaper:

Snake Found in Baby's Crib!

**Hospital Treats 50 Snake Bite
Victims in a Year!**

**Massive Power Outage
Caused by Snakes!**

**Snake Swallows Several Fingers
of a Baby's Hand!**

Do these events sound real? Believe it or not, all of these things happened on Guam. Guam is a beautiful, tiny island in the western Pacific Ocean.

Guam has a huge problem with brown tree snakes. They have caused trouble for the people of Guam for almost 60 years. Part of the problem is that the brown tree snake is not from Guam.

Snakes' Arrival

Scientists believe the brown tree snake arrived in Guam after World War II. They think the snakes crawled onto US military ships and stowed away in the cargo. When the cargo was dropped off in Guam, the snakes slithered out into the jungle.

Since the snake is not from Guam, it has no natural predator on the island. This means there is nothing to control the brown tree snake population.

A Fearsome Snake!

The brown tree snake has a fearsome appearance. It has black eyes with a yellow-green center. It can sometimes grow to a length of 10 feet!

The snakes are often found in boxes, houses, cars, and on airplanes. Some people in Guam say the snakes have even been found in their toilets!

Snake Problems

Perhaps the biggest problem caused by the brown tree snakes is power outages. The snakes like to climb up onto power lines and transformers. Then they are electrocuted and cause a short circuit. The short circuit cuts out the power to entire villages. It is estimated that these power outages cost millions each year.

The brown tree snake is not very dangerous to adults. But the brown tree snake's venom can make small children very ill. Also, its bite really hurts. Luckily, there have been no deaths in Guam due to brown tree snake bites.

Snakes Spread

Recently, brown tree snakes have been found on at least six other islands in the Pacific Ocean, such as Oahu, Hawaii. Once again, they are stowing away in boxes on air shipments or shipping cargo. Many people are concerned about the problem. The snake population in Guam is already out of control. Officials do not want this to happen on other Pacific islands.

But for now, the brown tree snake continues to slither its way up and down power lines, over and under cars and airplanes, and in and out of houses!

Brown Tree Snake Facts

Size: 18 inches at hatching 3 feet by
                 first year 8–10 feet as an adult

Weight: 5 pounds as an adult

Prey: Birds, lizards, small mammals,
                 eggs, household pets

Reproduction: 12 eggs once or twice a year
                 Eggs hatch 90 days later

Habitat: Trees and shrubs

Distribution: Native to Solomon Islands, New
                 Guinea, northern and eastern
                 Australia, and eastern Indonesia.
                 Invaded Guam during WWII.

Burmese Pythons Invade the Everglades

The brown tree snake is not the only snake to take over an area. Burmese pythons have invaded Everglades National Park!

Burmese pythons can grow larger than 20 feet long, weigh more than 200 pounds, and even overpower a grown man!

Burmese pythons do not have fangs. They are constrictors—the pythons suffocate their prey by wrapping their strong, muscular bodies around their victim, and slowly squeezing the life out of the animal.

Like the brown tree snake, Burmese pythons are not native to their new home. Scientists are struggling to stop the snake from taking over!

Guzman Stows Away on an Airplane—Twice

DATAFILE

Timeline

June 1993

Juan Guzman stows away on a plane from Colombia to Miami, Florida.

July 1993

Juan makes a second attempt to enter the United States on another plane.

Where is Colombia?

HERE

Key Terms

custody—to be in charge of and care for someone

deployed—sent out

oxygen—the gas we breathe to live

perseverance—the ability to keep on working toward one's goal

?

Did You Know?

Airplanes travel at more than 500 miles per hour at 30,000 feet, where the air is thin and temperatures are freezing. Many stowaways hidden on airplanes die because they freeze to death or run out of oxygen while the plane flies at such high altitude.

Guzman Stows Away on an Airplane—Twice

Juan Guzman's life was not easy. He was 17 years old and he lived in Colombia. Juan said his stepfather beat him. And Juan felt his mother did not want him anymore. Juan could not imagine his life getting any better.

Big Dreams

Juan had dreams of leaving Colombia. He wanted to study in Mexico. But mostly he was filled with thoughts of living in America. For Juan, living in America was the answer to all of his troubles.

Juan could not afford a plane ticket to America. He also could not get the visa he needed to enter America. Juan's only hope was to sneak into America.

A Dangerous Plan

Juan decided the best way to get to America was to stow away on an airplane. He learned that he could get into the wheel well of the plane's landing gear. There he thought he would be safe until the plane landed.

Juan's plan was dangerous enough to begin with. But it turned out to be even more risky than Juan could have imagined.

What Juan did not realize is that as a plane goes up into the sky, the air becomes very cold. Also, there is little oxygen to breathe. By all accounts, anyone who stowed away in the wheel well of an airplane should die during the flight.

Stow Away!

On June 4, 1993, Juan stowed away in the wheel well of a cargo jet loaded with flowers, just as he planned. Three hours later, the plane landed in Miami, Florida. Juan was still alive! He was almost free. But airport security officers found Juan before he could sneak away. He was quickly taken into custody.

Many people at the airport were angry with Juan for his reckless attempt. But they were even more amazed that he survived the flight at all. Previous attempts at stowing away in the wheel wells of airplanes had resulted in dead bodies falling from the planes when the landing gear deployed.

Juan gained a lot of attention for his daring attempt. At first, Juan told US authorities that he was an orphan. He spent more than a month among other Colombians living in Miami. He was a celebrity among them. Even though what Juan did was illegal, the Colombians admired his bravery. They welcomed him into their homes and gave him gifts.

Later, Juan told US authorities he had lied to them about being an orphan. On July 14, Juan was sent back to Colombia.

A Second Attempt

For most, this would be the end of the story. But for Juan Guzman, it was a second chance. Juan made another plan to get into America. He wasted no time. Less than two weeks later, Juan called friends he had made in Miami. He told them to be at the airport to pick him up on July 23 at 11 a.m.

This time Juan was better prepared. He would again stow away in the wheel well. He would stay warmer. He wore two pairs of pants, two shirts, and a sweater. Still, there was no reason to believe that he would survive this flight.

*"He said, 'Don't worry, I know what I'm doing...'
But he has that idea fixed in his head and no one
is going to take it away." — Berta Lozano*

The miracle happened again! Juan endured five take-offs and landings during a training flight. Eventually he landed safely in Miami. But Juan could not sneak out of the airport. Juan was discovered and arrested again.

A Dream Destroyed

Many people wanted to help Juan stay in America. However, Juan's actions were illegal in both America and Colombia. So it is unlikely now that Juan will ever be able to stay in the United States.

An airline worker checks the wheel wells of a plane for stowaways.

Colombia Facts

Bordered by: Panama on the northwest; Venezuela and Brazil on the east; Peru and Ecuador on the south

Capital: Bogotá

Area: 440,831 square miles

Named for: Christopher Columbus – The European explorer who discovered the Americas

Population: 42,310,775 (estimated in July 2004)

Life expectancy: Male 68 years; Female 75 years

Language: Spanish

Airports: 900+ (paved and unpaved)

Religion: Roman Catholic 90%

Colombia and Its Neighbors

*Edson Rojas Stows Away on a
Deadly Truck Trip*

DATAFILE

Timeline

July 2002

Edson Rojas almost dies while stowing away on a
tractor trailer.

May 2004

Edson recovers and attends school in Kansas.

Where is Mexico?

Key Terms

conscious—to be awake and aware of what is going on around you

sinister—evil; very negative

ventilation—a place where fresh air can get into a closed space

? Did You Know?

People who help Mexicans cross the border into America are often called human "coyotes." In Native American tales, coyotes are often portrayed as tricksters. Human "coyotes" prey on the desperation of others.

Edson Rojas Stows Away on a Deadly Truck Trip

There was no more water. There was no way out. There was no ventilation and the oxygen was running low. The temperature inside the truck had risen to 150 degrees!

> *"No quiero morir. (I don't want to die.)"*
> — *A Mexican immigrant aboard the truck*

Edson Rojas was barely conscious. He and more than 40 other Mexican immigrants had been in the tractor trailer for more than 12 hours. The rig hurtled down the highway in the afternoon heat. None of them knew if they would get out alive.

Dying of Thirst

When the truck came to a slow stop, those who could, pounded on the walls. The driver came around to the back and lifted the hatch. When he did, dozens of immigrants tumbled out of the trailer. They gasped for air and crawled on the ground. "Agua," they cried, looking for water.

Back inside the trailer, a few people still lingered. One of them was Edson. He could barely think or move his body. But something told him to move toward the light. Then, just as suddenly as it opened, the trailer slammed shut. The truck took off again.

In the light, Edson had made out the bodies of at least two others still in the trailer with him. But neither moved. Edson thought they were both dead. He did not have much hope for himself.

This One is Alive!

More than 50 miles later, the truck stopped again. This time, a state trooper opened the doors. He almost turned away at the smell of vomit, sweat, and urine. But then he saw the bodies. The trooper grabbed one boy's legs and felt for a pulse. There was none. He checked the second body. Again, there was none.

The trooper came to Edson expecting to find a third dead body. But then he noticed some movement. He put his ear to Edson's mouth and felt his breath.

> *"Hey! We've got one that's alive!"*
> *— Kam Pierce, Texas State Trooper*

The troopers rushed Edson to the hospital. He was close to death. Doctors gave him fluids and assisted his breathing.

Meanwhile, the police arrested the men driving the truck. Stowing away Mexican immigrants is illegal. Letting them overheat and die in a trailer is even worse. The drivers were in a lot of trouble.

Back at the hospital, Edson slowly recovered. He was glad to be alive. The US government allowed him to stay in the United States. He now lives in Kansas with his father. He plays soccer and goes to school.

But Edson also has bad memories of his adventure. Edson believes he would never try to stow away again.

*"I get very nervous when I get into a car...
I have a lot of nightmares."— Edson Rojas*

Body Heat Index

On average, more than 170 Americans die from heat stroke each year. Our bodies lose heat by sweating, changing how our blood circulates in our bodies, and, as a last resort, by panting when our body temperature reaches above 98.6 F.

Troopers estimate the temperature reached 150 degrees inside the tractor-trailer Edson Rojas and more than 40 other illegal immigrants were packed into. At this temperature, it is amazing Edson and most of the others made it out alive!

Body Heat Index and Heat Disorders

Heat Index (°F)	Heat Disorder
80°–90°	Fatigue
90°–105°	Heat cramps and heat exhaustion
105°–130°	Heat cramps, heat exhaustion, and heat stroke
130° or greater	Heat Stroke

Heat Index: the temperature we feel outdoors when heat and humidity combine

Fatigue: tiredness

Heat Cramps: muscle cramps and lots of sweating

Heat Exhaustion: weakness, dizziness, nausea, and lots of sweating

Heat Stroke: sweating stops, extremely high body temperature, and collapse

The US Citizenship and Immigration Services (USCIS)

The Immigration and Naturalization Service (INS) was created in 1933. With World War II looming, citizens saw immigration as a national security problem.

After World War II, the INS helped many people come to America. During the 1950s and 1960s, Americans became very concerned about Communists and organized crime rings. The INS investigated people and deported them.

In 2003, the INS was abolished. It was renamed US Immigration and Customs Enforcement (ICE). It is a part of the Department of Homeland Security (DHS).

The primary responsibility for the enforcement of immigration law within DHS rests with ICE and the US Customs and Border Protection (CBP).

Every person arriving by land, sea, and air is screened. Those who try to enter the United States illegally are deported.

From the DHS Annual Report

This report presents information on the apprehension, detention, return, and removal of foreign nationals during 2010.

- DHS apprehended 517,000 foreign nationals; 83 percent were natives of Mexico.

- ICE detained approximately 363,000 foreign nationals.

- DHS removed 387,000 foreign nationals from the United States.

- The leading countries of origin of those removed were Mexico (73 percent), Guatemala (8 percent), Honduras (6 percent), and El Salvador (5 percent).

- Reinstatements of final orders accounted for 131,000, or 34 percent, of all removals.

- Expedited removals accounted for 111,000, or 29 percent, of all removals.

- ICE removed 169,000 known criminal aliens from the United States.

- DHS returned 476,000 foreign nationals to their home countries without a removal order.

McKinley Ships Himself from New York to Texas
DATAFILE

Timeline

May 2003

President Bush declares an end to major combat in Iraq.

September 2003

Charles McKinley ships himself from New York to DeSoto, Texas.

Where is DeSoto, Texas?

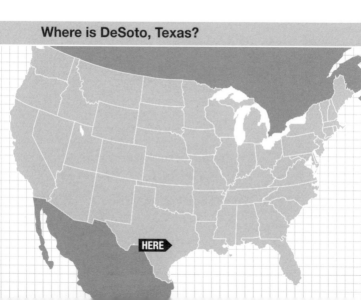

Key Terms

declare—to state publicly

unpressurized—a section of an airplane that has no oxygen and will not support humans

Did You Know?

Charles's ability to stowaway brought attention to security concerns at airports. As of August 2004, the Transportation Security Administration began testing cargo at three major US airports.

McKinley Ships Himself from New York to Texas

Charles McKinley had a problem. He felt lonely and homesick. Charles wanted to visit his parents in DeSoto, Texas. But he did not have enough money to get there.

Charles worked at a shipping company. A friend of Charles's had an idea: Charles could save money by shipping himself to Texas in a crate!

Surely, Charles had heard stories of stowaways. But he probably never thought he would be one! Charles was 25 years old and five feet, eight inches tall. Stuffed into a box three and a half feet wide and three feet tall, Charles would have been very uncomfortable.

A 15-Hour Journey

But on the morning of September 5, 2003, that's exactly what Charles did. His friend helped pack Charles into a wooden crate. The crate was supposed to contain computers and clothes. The $550 shipping fee was illegally charged to a company Charles worked with.

For the next 15 hours, Charles was stuck inside the crate with no food or water. He had a cell phone, but it did not work. At times, Charles got very scared.

"Oh God, I don't know why I'm doing this... any minute somebody will notice that there's somebody sitting inside this crate..."
— Charles McKinley

Charles also risked being placed in an unpressurized cargo hold. This would have meant there would have been little oxygen for him to breathe. Plus the temperature might have dropped so low that Charles could have frozen to death.

Safe on the Ground

More than 1,500 miles later, his plane landed in Dallas, Texas. Charles had survived so far. No one had noticed him yet.

A little while later, his crate was loaded onto a delivery truck. The truck drove to DeSoto, Texas, where his parents lived. The deliveryman thought he was dropping off computers and clothes. As he went to get the crate, he noticed a pair of eyes looking at him. At first, the deliveryman was stunned. He thought Charles was dead. He called the police.

Then Charles began prying himself out of the crate. Once he got out, he shook the deliveryman's hand and walked away. The deliveryman could not believe his eyes!

Caught!

Charles almost got away. By now the police were already on their way. When the police arrived, they wanted to know how Charles had gotten past airport security from New York to Dallas. They also wanted to arrest Charles because stowing away is illegal. He was in a lot of trouble.

A few months later, Charles was sentenced to a year of probation and a $1,500 fine. A regular flight from New York to Dallas costs around $240. In the end, it would have been cheaper for Charles to buy the ticket home.

"I don't like what you did. It was wrong and
stupid. But I'm glad you are standing here this
morning, rather than have met a fate much
worse by the stupidity of your actions."
— US Magistrate Judge Charles Bleil

Charles's actions also brought attention to se-curity problems at airports. Since September 11, 2001, airport officials have been very concerned about anyone getting onto an airplane illegally like Charles did. Many people were angry that Charles was not caught sooner. Since the incident, airports have continued to tighten their security.

The Price of Stowing Away

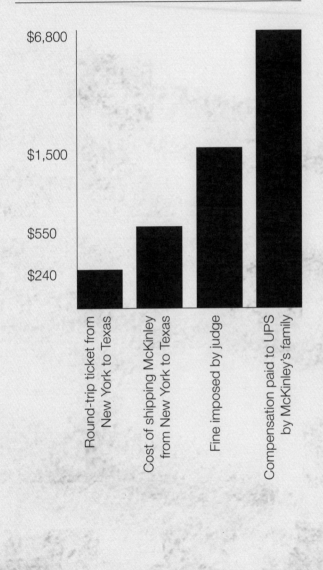

Woman Ships Herself to the United States

August 25, 2003: An unidentified Cuban woman shipped herself from the Bahamas to Miami in a crate about the size of a small filing cabinet.

A DHL cargo crew found the woman curled up inside the box after it was unloaded at Miami International Airport. She seemed happy and healthy.

US Immigration officials in Miami say the woman will be allowed to stay in the United States. The US government allows any Cubans who reach land to stay in the United States.

Officials are not saying how long the young woman was in the box, but she is lucky to be alive.

Busy Airports Test Cargo

August 2004: The Transportation Security Administration began testing cargo at three of the nation's busiest airports: Atlanta, Dallas-Fort Worth, and Miami.

The tests will see if machines that detect explosives in luggage can be used to scan cargo before it is placed on passenger aircraft. Most often, bomb-sniffing dogs check some, but not all, cargo transported by plane.

These new measures still would not find stowaways like Charles McKinley. However, using them should make our airlines safer

H1N1 Global Pandemic
DATAFILE

Timeline

1918–1919

The Spanish flu pandemic kills millions as it spreads throughout the world.

1968–1969

The Hong Kong flu first entered the United States from soldiers returning from the war in Vietnam.

2009

The H1N1 virus was initially called swine flu.

Where is Vietnam?

Key Terms

contagious—likely to transmit a disease through contact with other people or animals

immune system—a collection of organs, cells, and tissues that work together to protect your body from disease

mutate—change or cause to change in form or nature

?

Did You Know?

The states of Wisconsin, Texas, and Illinois experienced the highest rate of H1N1 infection. Worldwide, the countries most affected were Germany, Portugal, and China.

H1N1 Global Pandemic

Every time you sneeze, you release tiny droplets of water into the air. The same is true when you cough. It is these tiny droplets that spread influenza. This disease is commonly known as the flu.

That's why it's good to get a flu shot and wash your hands often. But that's not always enough. The virus is very contagious.

Influenza is an infectious disease that spreads among birds and mammals. People are mammals. But they are not affected by certain strains of flu. Some strains affect people but not other animals.

Flu is more serious than the common cold. Fever, cough, sore throat, and muscle pains are common flu symptoms. Others include headache, weakness, and general discomfort.

By contrast, symptoms of the common cold are sneezing and a runny or stuffy nose. They may also include a cough, headache, or sore throat. But if you have a fever, it's probably something more serious than a cold.

Seasonal flu strikes every year. It affects people when the weather gets cold. Seasonal flu kills 250,000 to 500,000 people worldwide every year.

Generally, those who die from seasonal flu are the very young or very old. People with weakened immune systems are also more likely to die from flu. One example is people with HIV or AIDS. Cancer patients are another.

In 2009, swine flu struck. It was a pandemic. An epidemic is when more people than expected get sick. A pandemic is when a huge number of people—or people throughout the world—get sick. The 2009 swine flu pandemic spread throughout the world.

There were three pandemics in the 20th century: the Spanish flu, the Asian flu, and the Hong Kong flu. Altogether they killed tens of millions of people worldwide.

The Spanish flu pandemic of 1918–1919 was by far the worst. In fact, it was one of the worst natural disasters in history. A third of the world's population was infected. Between 50 and 130 million people died. This was 3 to 6 percent of the entire world's population.

The Spanish flu was very different from seasonal flu. Seasonal flu attacks people with weakened immune systems. But the Spanish flu attacked healthy young adults. It caused their immune systems to overreact while trying to fight the virus. This "friendly fire" reaction often resulted in death.

The other two pandemics in the 20th century were the Asian flu and the Hong Kong flu. The Asian flu struck in 1957. It killed from one to two million people worldwide. The Hong Kong flu killed from one to four million in 1968–69.

Each pandemic was caused by a new strain of flu virus. New strains appear when an existing virus mutates. That's when a cell changes form. When a new virus appears, our bodies have to learn how to fight it.

So when a new strain pops up, doctors worry. A really bad pandemic could kill millions of people.

The 2009 swine flu pandemic was the second time the H1N1 virus popped up. The first time was the Spanish flu pandemic in 1918. The 2009 pandemic was caused by the same virus, but it had mutated.

The World Health Organization (WHO) was extremely concerned. Many millions of people died in the 1918 Spanish flu pandemic. The WHO thought it could happen again with swine flu. And the world's population is much larger today. So they thought the swine flu pandemic might be even worse.

Swine flu got its name from pigs. The 2009 H1N1 virus was a mixture. It came from bird, swine, and human flu viruses. They were also combined with a Eurasian pig flu virus. The 2009 H1N1 virus was the first time pig, bird, and human viruses combined into one.

Some people believed pigs were responsible. The Egyptian government even ordered the slaughter of every pig in Egypt in 2009. And many countries banned the import of American pork products.

The WHO has stated that eating pork does not transmit swine flu. However, the first instance of this strain of H1N1 was found on a factory pig farm in North Carolina in 1998. Large factory farms can have unclean conditions. Animals live too close together and are given lots of antibiotics. Flu can spread very quickly under these conditions.

With the H1N1 virus, many of the people who died had secondary infections. The secondary infections were caused by bacteria rather than the

This is a small-scale pig farm. There are three main flu viruses found in pigs in the US, H1N1, H3N2, and H1N2.

H1N1 virus. After a few days of flu symptoms, a person will start to feel better. Then all of a sudden the fever comes back, and they get much worse.

In 2003, there was an epidemic of bird flu that nearly became a pandemic. When the 2009 swine flu became a pandemic, the WHO was on alert. The WHO is still trying to determine exactly how many people died from H1N1.

The Case of the Huanglongbing
DATAFILE

Timeline

1920s

Huanglongbing (HLB) is first recognized damaging citrus crops in China.

1981

California spends over $40 million fighting the Mediterranean fruit fly infestation.

2005

HLB is discovered in Florida citrus crops.

Where is China?

HERE

Key Terms

bacterial infection—detrimental colonization of a host organism by a foreign parasite species

psyllid—any of various jumping plant lice that feed on plant juices

quarantine—a place of isolation where people or animals are placed when they have been exposed to infectious or contagious diseases

revenue—income

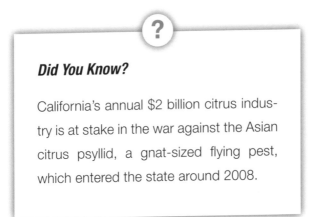

Did You Know?

California's annual $2 billion citrus industry is at stake in the war against the Asian citrus psyllid, a gnat-sized flying pest, which entered the state around 2008.

The Case of the Huanglongbing

Many Americans love drinking orange juice with their breakfast. We tend to take it for granted. But that may not be the case for much longer.

A disease called huanglongbing (HLB) is threatening the world's citrus fruits. These include oranges, tangerines, grapefruit, lemons, and limes, among others. Sweet oranges and mandarins suffer the disease more than lemons and grapefruit do.

Huanglongbing is a Chinese word meaning "yellow shoot disease." Yellow shoots are a symptom of the disease. Shoots are the tiny sprouts of a new plant. Yellow shoots equal a sick plant.

HLB is also called "citrus greening." That's because fruits on affected trees stay partly green. They are lopsided and taste bitter. These fruits are no good for eating or even juicing.

The disease is caused by bacteria. It is spread by tiny insects called Asian citrus psyllids. These winged insects are only about one-eighth of an inch long.

Asian citrus psyllids suck the sap or juice out of citrus leaves. In doing so, they deposit HLB bacteria. Citrus plants die from both the insect damage and the bacteria. But it is mostly the bacterial infection that kills citrus.

Trees infected with HLB die within a few years. There is no cure.

This lemon tree branch is loaded with fresh fruit. Someday there may be no more lemons because trees may die from "yellow shoot disease," or huanglongbing, a worldwide citrus epidemic.

HLB first started to affect citrus crops in China in the 1920s. It is now present in every Asian country but Japan. In the late 1940s, it appeared in Africa. Today it affects just about every citrus growing region in the world.

In 1998, Asian citrus psyllids were discovered in Florida. And in 2005, the first HLB-diseased tree was found there. Today the disease is affecting trees in every citrus-growing county in Florida.

So far there have been over 7,000 jobs lost in Florida due to HLB. Growers have lost $1.3 billion in revenue.

There is a massive research effort underway. Scientists are trying to find a way to beat HLB. So far they have not had much luck.

The damage is spreading fast. A solution needs to be found soon. Otherwise, Florida's $9.3 billion citrus industry could be lost.

Pesticides can kill the Asian citrus psyllids, but there is no treatment for the HLB infection. Some scientists say genetic modification is the only answer. That's when DNA from one organism is mixed with that of another. That could mean putting apple DNA into a tomato, for instance.

Crops that are genetically modified are called GMO. That stands for genetically modified organism. An organism is any living being. Organisms include everything from bacteria and viruses to goats and cows—even people.

Researchers have developed many genetically modified citrus trees. They are trying to find out which modifications will work against HLB. So far, introducing two spinach genes into grapefruit trees seems to be effective.

It will take years for this modification to go through the USDA regulation process. But so far scientists have found no other solution. Only time will tell.

Meanwhile, HLB has spread to other parts of the United States. Once HLB is found, the surrounding area is quarantined. This means no one can bring citrus plants in or out.

So far the entire states of Alabama, Florida, Georgia, Hawaii, Louisiana, Mississippi, and Texas have been quarantined.

In March 2012, the first case of HLB was confirmed in California. A hybrid lemon/pommelo tree in Hacienda Heights was confirmed to be infected. The tree was in a residential yard in Los Angeles County.

Citrus trees are a staple in Southern California. Many people have oranges or lemons growing in their yards. That could become a thing of the past unless a solution is found.

Once the insect is discovered in a new area, the disease usually follows a few years later. For instance, in California, the first Asian citrus psyllid was found in 2008. The disease appeared in 2012.

A good defense is to keep the psyllids away. People with citrus trees should keep a close eye on them.

The first thing to look for is eggs. Asian citrus psyllid eggs are bright yellow-orange. They are almond-shaped and appear in groups. The eggs are found on the newest, unfolded leaves.

When the eggs hatch, the baby insects are called nymphs. They don't have wings yet. They are flat and have red eyes and waxy white tubes sticking out of their backs. Nymphs leave sooty mold on the leaves.

Adults are small brown insects with wings. They are tiny—about one-eighth of an inch long. They feed with their heads down.

People who think their trees might be infected should report it immediately to their states's department of agriculture.

Hawaii's Endangered Honeycreepers
DATAFILE

Timeline

1844

The last two known great auks are brutally killed.

1927

The paradise parrot of Australia is declared extinct after years of habitat loss and over-hunting.

1987

On the Hawaiian island of Kauai, the tiny Kaua'i 'O'o bird becomes extinct.

Where are the Hawaiian Islands?

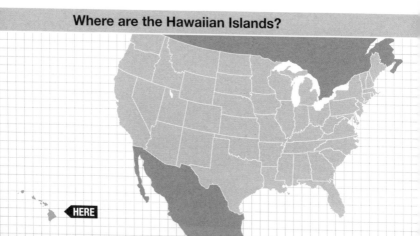

HERE

Key Terms

biodiversity—variety of life in the world or in a particular habitat or ecosystem

conservationist—person who advocates or acts for the protection and preservation of the environment and wildlife

habitat—natural home or environment of an animal, plant, or other organism

predator—an animal that hunts and eats other animals

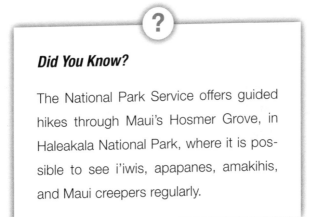

Did You Know?

The National Park Service offers guided hikes through Maui's Hosmer Grove, in Haleakala National Park, where it is possible to see i'iwis, apapanes, amakihis, and Maui creepers regularly.

Hawaii's Endangered Honeycreepers

Life on earth is very diverse. There are many different species of plants and animals.

Sometimes a species goes extinct, or dies out. Animals that have recently become extinct include the Western black rhino (2011), the Miss Waldron's red colobus monkey (2000), and the golden toad (1988). There have been many others.

When a species becomes extinct, there's a ripple effect. For instance, if there were no more spiders, insects would take over. That's because spiders eat bugs. Or if all the bees died, flowers could not be pollinated. Then there would be no more fruits or vegetables.

People have done some very stupid things to our planet. They have caused many species to go extinct. This upsets the delicate balance of life.

One example of a species that humans killed off is the passenger pigeon. The very last one died in 1914. It was a passenger pigeon named Martha. She died in the Cincinnati Zoo on September 1, 1914.

Just 100 years before that, passenger pigeons were the most common bird in the United States.

Passenger pigeons flew in huge flocks of hundreds of thousands of birds. It could take hours for a flock to fly over an area. But they were hunted to extinction. Deforestation was also a factor. That's when forests are chopped down to clear land for farming or to harvest wood.

Scientists learned a lesson from the passenger pigeon. They learned that it is indeed possible for a common species to go extinct. Can you imagine if all the sparrows were gone? What would our world be like with no more bees?

Sad to say, humans are still killing off other species today. We are polluting our planet's air and water. And we are cutting down forests and destroying habitats.

Modern scientists are working to make up for this damage. They are helping these endangered species. That's a species whose numbers have dropped to the point of near-extinction.

When a species becomes endangered, scientists do all they can to help it come back. They understand how important biodiversity is. Biodiversity means the variety of life in a habitat. It is like a very complicated puzzle. Taking one part out affects all the others.

Currently there are about eight or nine million species on earth. That includes plants and animals as well as bacteria and viruses. It includes everything from worms and grass to ants, lions, mold, dragonflies, roses, and clams.

Of these eight or nine million species, about 9,000 to 10,000 are birds. And of these birds, 22 species are Hawaiian honeycreepers. These songbirds are endemic to Hawaii. That means it is the only place on earth where they live.

Many species of honeycreepers have already gone extinct. At one point, there were at least 51 species of Hawaiian honeycreepers. Today there are only 22.

Some of the most endangered honeycreepers are the akikiki, the Maui parrotbill, and the nukupuu. Of these, the nukupuu may already be extinct.

Honeycreepers are members of the finch family. Like other finches, they are small enough to fit in your hand. They range in color from bright yellow to scarlet red.

Some of these colorful songbirds have long, curved beaks. This allows them to drink nectar out of flowers or to bore into wood for insects. Other honeycreepers have straight, thin bills for catching insects. Yet others have wedge-shaped bills like finches. These honeycreepers eat seeds.

Honeycreepers are very sensitive to their habitat. That's the area where they live.

One of the main things harming honeycreepers is mosquitoes. They carry avian malaria—a disease that kills birds. Five endangered honeycreeper species have moved to higher elevations. Mosquitoes don't live high in the mountains. It is not warm enough. The honeycreepers are less likely to get sick.

Some of Hawaii's honeycreepers can be seen at Hosmer Grove (elevation 7,000 feet), just inside Haleakala National Park.

But climate change is increasing the temperatures at higher elevations. And the mosquitoes are moving up too. Hawaii is working on reducing their wild pig and goat population. Mosquitoes feed on them. They hope to drastically reduce mosquitoes with this plan.

Another problem is ungulates, or hoofed animals. Pigs and goats are not native to Hawaii. They were brought here by people many years ago. The pigs and goats also hurt the honeycreepers by destroying the plants the birds feed on by stripping away the tender leaves.

Predators, too, were brought by people. Cats, rats, and mongooses eat honeycreepers.

Captive breeding is another way people can help the honeycreepers. Pairs of birds are kept in zoos and helped to have babies. Then the young birds are released into the wild when they are old enough.

The problem with captive breeding is that the honeycreepers' habitat is disappearing. There just isn't as much forested area with the kind of flowers and trees they like. So conservationists are working to preserve habitat. These people care about wildlife and want it to thrive.

There is hope, though. The Amakihi is one kind of honeycreeper that is not endangered. This bird has evolved to be resistant to malaria. And it has learned to adapt to habitat destruction.

Hopefully other honeycreeper species will do the same. In the meantime, conservationists are doing all they can to help.

Haena Hanalei KAUAI

Mana Lihue

NIIHAU

Wahiawa OAH

Makaha

Honolulu

K

Hawaii

More than half of the 56 types of honeycreeper in the Hawaiian Islands is extinct. Because of Hawaii's isolation

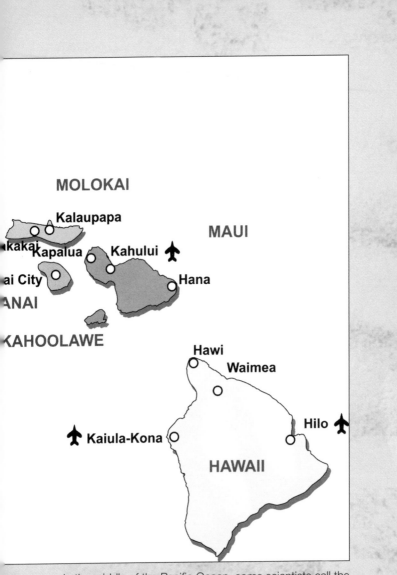

in the middle of the Pacific Ocean, some scientists call the islands a "blank slate" for evolution.

Glossary

bacterial infection—detrimental colonization of a host organism by a foreign parasite species

biodiversity—variety of life in the world or in a particular habitat or ecosystem

cargo—goods transported in planes, trucks, ships, etc.

colony—a region ruled by another country

conscious—to be awake and aware of what is going on around you

conservationist—person who advocates or acts for the protection and preservation of the environment and wildlife

contagious—likely to transmit a disease through contact with other people or animals

custody—to be in charge of and care for someone

declare—to state publicly

deployed—sent out

disfigured—deeply scarred, having the appearance spoiled

estimate—to make an informed guess about a measurement

expedition—a group of people working together to make a discovery

habitat—natural home or environment of an animal, plant, or other organism

immune system—a collection of organs, cells, and tissues that work together to protect your body from disease

mutate—change or cause to change in form or nature

nuisance—an annoying problem

oxygen—the gas we breathe to live

perseverance—the ability to keep on working toward one's goal

predator—an animal that hunts and eats other animals

psyllid—any of various jumping plant lice that feed on plant juices

quarantine—a place of isolation where people or animals are placed when they have been exposed to infectious or contagious diseases

rebellious—to act out against those in authority

revenue—income

sinister—evil; very negative

slither—to slide; to move like a snake

unpressurized—a section of an airplane that has no oxygen and will not support humans

ventilation—a place where fresh air can get into a closed space

Index